SKUNKS
at Night

Kathleen A. Klatte

PowerKiDS press
New York

Published in 2021 by The Rosen Publishing Group, Inc.
29 East 21st Street, New York, NY 10010

First Edition

Portions of this work were originally authored by Doreen Gonzales and published as *Skunks in the Dark*. All new material in this edition authored by Kathleen A. Klatte.

Editor: Kathleen Klatte
Book Design: Michael Flynn

Photo Credits: Cover, p. 22 Eric Isselee/Shutterstock.com; (series background) MoreThanPicture/Shutterstock.com; p. 5 Geoffrey Kuchera/Shutterstock.com; p. 6 Martin Belli/Shutterstock.com; pp. 7, 17 Agnieszka Bacal/Shutterstock.com; p. 8 Bildagentur Zoonar GmbH/Shutterstock.com; p. 9 Sumbul/Shutterstock.com; p. 11 Kerry Hargrove/Shutterstock.com; p. 12 Debbie Steinhausser/Shutterstock.com; p. 13 J & C Sohns/Picture Press/Getty Images; p. 15 S.J. Krasemann/Photolibrary/Getty Images; p. 18 Fall-line Photography/Shutterstock.com; p. 19 Sean R. Stubben/Shutterstock.com; p. 21 Daniel; J. Cox/Oxford Scientific/Getty Images.

Cataloging-in-Publication Data

Names: Klatte, Kathleen A.
Title: Skunks at night / Kathleen A. Klatte.
Description: New York : PowerKids Press, 2021. | Series: Up all night! nocturnal animals | Includes glossary and index.
Identifiers: ISBN 9781725318854 (pbk.) | ISBN 9781725318878 (library bound) | ISBN 9781725318861 (6 pack)
Subjects: LCSH: Skunks–Juvenile literature. | Nocturnal animals–Juvenile literature.
Classification: LCC QL737.C248 K48 2021 | DDC 599.76'8–dc23

Some of the images in this book illustrate individuals who are models. The depictions do not imply actual situations or events.

Manufactured in the United States of America

CPSIA Compliance Information: Batch #CSPK20. For Further Information contact Rosen Publishing, New York, New York at 1-800-237-9932.

Find us on

CONTENTS

STINKY, STRIPED VISITORS

Even though many people know skunks for their awful-smelling spray, they aren't just smelly pests. Many skunks eat things humans don't like, such as **insects** that harm crops. Other skunks eat rats and mice.

Skunks are small, furry **mammals**. Most skunks are black and white. The largest skunks are about 30 inches (76.2 cm) long and weigh about 14 pounds (6.4 kg). All skunks have short legs, and most skunks have long, fluffy tails. Skunks are mostly nocturnal, which means they're active mainly at night. However, some skunks are crepuscular, which means they're active at **twilight**.

WHILE YOU'RE SLEEPING

The Latin name for skunk means "bad odor." However, skunks give plenty of warning, and they generally don't spray unless they're cornered or **threatened**.

IT'S ALWAYS BEST TO LEAVE WILD ANIMALS ALONE. IF YOU GIVE THEM PLENTY OF SPACE, THEY'LL RUN AWAY WITHOUT BOTHERING YOU.

STRIPES AND SPOTS

There are 11 different species, or kinds, of skunks. Nine types are familiar to people in North America. Most are black and white and about the size of a housecat.

One of the most common skunks is the striped skunk. These skunks are black with two white stripes down their back. Striped skunks also have a white stripe on their face.

Hooded skunks, which look a lot like striped skunks, live in Mexico and in the southern United States. There are also hog-nosed skunks and spotted skunks. Spotted skunks are about the size of squirrels. Their white stripes swirl around their bodies.

SPOTTED SKUNKS ARE KNOWN FOR DOING A HANDSTAND AS PART OF A WARNING DISPLAY. IF WHATEVER'S BOTHERING THE SKUNK DOESN'T BACK OFF, IT'S IN FOR A SMELLY SURPRISE!

7

WHERE DO THEY LIVE?

Like many other kinds of animals, skunks tend to live close to a water supply. Some skunks like to live in fields near woods. Skunks often live in underground homes where rabbits or foxes once lived. Female skunks will sometimes live together in colder **habitats**. Skunks may also live in old logs or rock piles. These are safe places where skunks can sleep all day while other animals are out looking for food.

A HOLLOW LOG CAN MAKE A VERY GOOD HOME FOR A FAMILY OF SKUNKS. THEIR DARK FUR BLENDS INTO THE SHADOWS INSIDE THE LOG.

Skunks also often live near people. They make homes under buildings so people can't find them. Sometimes skunks live in **abandoned** buildings.

SOLITARY LIFE

Skunks tend to be **solitary** animals. They leave their homes each evening to hunt. Some skunks stay out all night looking for food. Others return to their dens after a while to rest until early morning.

In the winter, skunks sometimes stay in group dens. These keep them warm. A den can have as many as 20 skunks in it! Generally, female skunks spend most of the cold months sleeping, but male skunks sometimes go out looking for food if the weather turns warm. In the spring, skunks leave the group den to live alone again. A skunk uses up much of its body's stored food during winter.

WHILE YOU'RE SLEEPING

There's a common myth that a skunk out during the day must be sick. While you should never approach any wild animal, the skunk is most likely just looking for food.

SKUNKS LIKE TO TAKE OVER DENS THAT WERE BUILT BY ANOTHER ANIMAL. THEY'LL ONLY DIG THEIR OWN IF THERE'S NOTHING ELSE AVAILABLE.

BABY SKUNKS

Like many other animals, skunks give birth in the spring. Baby skunks are called kits. A mother has between 1 and 10 kits at a time. Newborn skunks can't see or hear, so they need their mother to give them food and keep them safe. The kits drink their mother's milk and stay in their den for about eight weeks. During this time, mother skunks keep other animals, such as predators, away from their dens. Sometimes, they even keep the father skunks away!

Kits are ready to have their own babies when they are 10 to 12 months old. Wild skunks generally live about three years.

THIS BABY SKUNK IS READY TO EXPLORE
THE WORLD OUTSIDE ITS DEN.

WHAT'S FOR DINNER?

Skunks eat both plants and animals. In fact, they'll eat just about any kind of food they can find. This makes them **omnivores**. They eat fruit, frogs, fish, bird eggs, and small mammals. Skunks also eat a lot of insects and mice.

Most skunks don't see very well in the daytime. Their sight is even worse at night. Therefore, skunks use hearing and smell to find food. Skunks can smell insects that are under the ground. Skunks are very good at digging up their dinner. Small skunks can fit into small spaces to catch mice and rats.

WHILE YOU'RE SLEEPING

Skunks sometimes get into trouble with people. Their claws are very good for digging up bugs and grubs. People get mad if their lawn is full of holes!

THIS SKUNK IS EATING A WASP'S NEST. SKUNKS EAT MANY THINGS THAT BOTHER PEOPLE.

A SMELLY DEFENSE

Being nocturnal is one of a skunk's best **defenses**. When skunks go out at night, their dark colors help them blend in and hide from nighttime hunters.

Skunks also keep predators away by spraying them with their musk. Musk is a smelly liquid that comes from under a skunk's tail. When a predator comes near, a skunk raises its tail, stamps its feet, and hisses like a cat. Sometimes, a skunk does a handstand! By doing these things, the skunk tells the predator to go away. If the predator stays, the skunk sprays the animal with musk. Skunks can point their face and tail at their **target** at the same time, ensuring good aim.

A SKUNK THAT'S BEING CHASED CAN SPRAY A CLOUD OF MUSK BEHIND IT. THIS CAN BE ENOUGH TO MAKE A PREDATOR GIVE UP.

17

SKUNK ON THE MENU

Some animals will brave the smell to catch skunks. Red-tailed hawks, foxes, coyotes, and bobcats are all hunters that eat skunks. Pet dogs will also hunt skunks sometimes. Some of the skunk's worst enemies are large owls, which are great nocturnal hunters.

WHILE YOU'RE SLEEPING

Skunks aren't the only animals whose coloring serves as a warning to predators. Ladybugs, monarch butterflies, and poison dart frogs all have coloring that reminds other animals that they're not good to eat.

THIS IS A HOG-NOSED SKUNK. IT'S EASY TO SEE HOW IT GOT THE NAME!

Most animals that have been sprayed by skunks learn to leave them alone so they won't get sprayed again. The animals remember the skunk's black-and-white markings and stay away. Owls don't have a sense of smell, so

PEOPLE, PETS, AND SKUNKS

Getting sprayed by a skunk is no fun. The smell of musk stays on people and animals for days. It often takes a special soap from a pet store to get rid of the smell.

Skunks can cause other problems, too. Sometimes, they get into trash cans or dig holes in lawns. Also, skunks can carry rabies, which is a very bad sickness. Skunks can pass rabies to other animals and to people through a bite. Without the right medicine, a person or animal can die from rabies. It's always best to stay away from wild animals.

THIS DOG MIGHT END UP WITH A VERY SMELLY SURPRISE! YOU SHOULD KEEP YOUR DOG ON A LEASH IF THERE

21

SKUNKS ARE OUR FRIENDS

Sometimes people don't like skunks because they don't know enough about them. For example, people sometimes think that skunks are getting into their trash when another animal is to blame. Many people also think that a skunk that's out during the day must have rabies. This isn't true.

Many people like skunks, though. Some people even keep them as pets. These special skunks are fixed so that they can't spray musk. Other people know that skunks eat insects and mice that bother people and eat crops. Like all animals, skunks are an important part of the natural world.

GLOSSARY

abandoned: Left to fall into a state of disuse.

defense: A feature of a living thing that helps keep it safe.

habitat: The natural home for plants, animals, and other living things.

insect: A small animal that has six legs and a body formed of three parts and that may have wings.

mammal: A warm-blooded animal that has a backbone and hair, breathes air, and feeds milk to its young.

omnivore: An animal that eats both plants and other animals.

solitary: Tending to live or spend time alone.

target: A place, thing, or person at which an attack is aimed.

threatened: Likely to be harmed.

twilight: The period when day is ending, and night is beginning.

WEBSITES

Due to the changing nature of Internet links, PowerKids Press has developed an online list of websites related to the subject of this book. This site is updated regularly. Please use this